RABBIT RUNDOWN: A DATA ENGINEERS GUIDE TO RABBITATS, RABBITOLOGY, AND RABBITISMS

First edition. August 4, 2023.

Copyright © 2023 W.

ISBN: 979-8223972754

Written by W.

-W-

602-365-0711
ucanbillme@pm.me   14,800 words.
BEE GOLDEN PUBLISHING LLC
3242 NE 3rd Avenue #1064
CAMAS, WA 98607

RABBIT RUNDOWN: A DATA ENGINEER'S GUIDE TO RABBITATS, RABBITOLOGY, AND RABBITISMS

by

<W>

Chapter 1: An Introduction to Rabbit Anatomy and Physiology

As mammals belonging to the Lagomorpha order, rabbits are fascinating creatures, intricately designed by nature's craft. Their anatomical structure and physiological functions are unique, making them an interesting subject of study.

Begin with the rabbit's skeleton. Compact and lightweight, it accounts for only 8% of their total body weight. The rabbit's skeletal system comprises the axial skeleton (skull, vertebral column, and rib cage) and the appendicular skeleton (limbs). Of interest is their remarkably robust hind legs, built for speed and agility, ideal for swift escapes from predators. Rabbits are digitigrades; they walk on their toes, adding to their sprinting prowess.

On their skull, two signature long ears dominate, serving more than just auditory purposes. Apart from hearing sounds over long distances, the extensive network of blood vessels in their ears helps in thermoregulation, dispersing heat and maintaining body temperature.

Beneath the fur, rabbits possess a double-layered coat – a longer, outer layer of guard hairs for protection, and a soft, dense undercoat for insulation. The pelage's color and pattern, governed by genetics, offer effective camouflage in their natural habitats.

Their cardiovascular system, built for survival, operates at high speeds, with a resting heart rate of approximately 180-300 beats per minute. The rabbit's respiratory system works closely with the cardiovascular system, maintaining a rapid rate of 30-60 breaths per minute. It's a delicate balance, as rabbits are obligate nasal breathers; they can only breathe through their noses.

A rabbit's vision deserves special mention. Positioned on either side of the head, their eyes provide a nearly panoramic field of view, optimal for detecting predators. They have a blind spot directly in front of their nose, but their impressive lateral vision compensates for this.

The digestive system of a rabbit is complex and highly specialized, reflecting their herbivorous diet. Their teeth – a set of incisors for cutting and molars for grinding plant material – grow continuously throughout their life. Behind the scenes, the rabbit's large caecum hosts a symbiotic microbial population that helps break down tough plant fibers into more easily digestible substances. It's crucial to note that rabbits practice caecotrophy - they re-ingest special fecal pellets (cecotropes) to absorb essential nutrients their body couldn't process the first time.

Rabbits have a unique reproductive system too. Females, or does, are induced ovulators - they ovulate in response to copulation rather than a cyclic rhythm. This aspect, combined with a short gestation period of around 31 days, allows rabbits to have multiple litters in a year.

To fully appreciate rabbits, one must dive deep into their biology. Their anatomical and physiological traits are evolutionary responses to the environment they inhabit and the ecological niche they fill. Each aspect, whether it's their powerful hind legs, specialized digestive system, or unique reproductive strategy, tells a story of adaptation and survival.

Let's delve further into rabbit anatomy, taking a closer look at their sensory systems.

Rabbits' large, upright ears do more than listen for distant rustling; they're also a key element in thermoregulation. Their ears contain a vast network of blood vessels, and by controlling blood flow through these vessels, rabbits can either retain or dissipate heat, regulating their body temperature in different environmental conditions. This is crucial for an animal that wears a fur coat year-round!

Their olfactory sense, too, is highly developed. A rabbit's nasal cavity is divided into two chambers - the main olfactory chamber and an additional one called the vomeronasal organ (or Jacobson's organ). These structures are laden with olfactory receptors that can detect a wide range of chemical signals, vital for communication, recognizing food, and sensing danger.

In terms of vision, rabbits have a well-adapted system for crepuscular life - being most active during twilight hours of dawn and dusk. They have a higher proportion of rod cells in their retina, aiding in low-light vision, and a tapetum lucidum, a layer of tissue behind the retina that reflects light back through it, increasing the light available to the photoreceptors.

Moving to their dental system, a rabbit's teeth are uniquely suited to their diet of fibrous plant material. They possess a set of continually growing incisors (two on top and two below), sharp and strong, for gnawing plant stems. Behind a gap called a diastema, they have a set of molars for grinding food into a pulp. The perpetual growth of their teeth is counterbalanced by the wear they experience from their diet, necessitating a constant supply of appropriate chewing material to prevent dental issues.

Their digestive system is a testament to evolutionary adaptation. The rabbit's stomach is simple and has a high pH to resist plant toxins. The small intestine is where most nutrient absorption occurs. The large intestine, including the caecum, is specialized for fermentation of plant material. Microorganisms in the caecum break down indigestible cellulose into volatile fatty acids, which can then be absorbed and used for energy.

The urinary system of rabbits, consisting of the kidneys, ureters, urinary bladder, and urethra, works hand in hand with the liver to detoxify the body and maintain electrolyte and water balance. Their kidneys are well adapted to conserve water, producing a highly concentrated urine.

Lastly, the reproductive system of rabbits is well suited to their prolific breeding. Female rabbits have a duplex uterus, with two separate uterine horns and no uterine body. This allows them to carry multiple pregnancies at different stages, contributing to their high reproductive rate.

Understanding a rabbit's intricate anatomy and physiology provides valuable insight into their behavior, care, and management. It highlights their remarkable adaptations to thrive in diverse environments, from meadows to our homes, showcasing the resilient versatility of nature.

Chapter 2: Rabbit Behavior and Social Structure

Rabbits exhibit a wide range of behaviors and social structures that are intrinsically tied to their survival in the wild and provide valuable insights for their domestic care.

Rabbits are crepuscular, most active during the twilight hours of dawn and dusk when their natural predators are least likely to be active. This crepuscular behavior pattern reduces their risk of predation and allows them to forage safely. They spend their day time resting in burrows or dense vegetation, coming out only when they perceive the environment to be safe.

One of the most distinctive behaviors of rabbits is thumping or drumming. When a rabbit thumps its hind legs, it is communicating alarm to other rabbits. This behavior can also be observed in domestic rabbits when they feel threatened or anxious.

Rabbits also display a joyous behavior known as binkying. When a rabbit binkies, it will jump into the air, twist its body and flick its feet. This is usually a sign of happiness and contentment.

In the wild, rabbits exhibit a social structure known as colonial living. They form social groups, often consisting of a dominant male, several females, and their offspring. The dominant male, also known as the buck, defends his territory and mates with the females, also known as does. This social structure provides safety in numbers and improves their chances of survival against predators.

The social hierarchy is also maintained through grooming behaviors, with the dominant rabbit usually being groomed by the subordinate members. This reinforces social bonds and helps maintain group harmony.

Rabbits communicate through a variety of subtle physical cues. They use their ears, nose, and tail to indicate their mood and intentions. For example, a relaxed rabbit will have its ears laid back and its body stretched out, while an alert rabbit will have its ears perked up and its body tense.

Understanding rabbit behavior and social structures can help in their domestic care. Providing them with opportunities for social interaction, ensuring a safe and comfortable environment, and recognizing signs of stress or illness are all critical aspects of responsible rabbit care.

Rabbits are more than just their physical anatomy and physiology. Their behavior, social structures, and ability to communicate offer a fascinating insight into their world. Whether in the wild or at home, understanding these aspects can lead to a better appreciation and care for these remarkable creatures.

Delving further into rabbit behavior, you will find that these creatures exhibit a sophisticated range of behaviors indicative of their intelligence and social complexity.

Foraging forms a significant part of a rabbit's day. Rabbits are herbivores, eating a diet consisting predominantly of grass, hay, and leafy greens, supplemented by fruits and vegetables. They exhibit 'grazing' behavior, eating small amounts throughout their active hours, which aids in constant wear of their ever-growing teeth and helps keep their complex digestive system running smoothly.

Rabbits are instinctive diggers, an aspect linked to their wild counterparts who dig extensive burrow systems, or 'warrens,' for shelter and safety. This instinct can often be observed in domestic rabbits too, who may dig into soft furnishings or garden soil.

Mutual grooming or 'allogrooming' is another key aspect of rabbit behavior, often observed within bonded pairs or groups. Grooming helps establish and reinforce social bonds, maintain hygiene, and provide comfort. Notably, the dominant rabbit is typically groomed more often by the submissive one.

In terms of defensive behavior, apart from thumping, rabbits may also exhibit 'boxing' when they feel threatened, standing on their hind legs and using their forepaws as if to box. They can bite and kick if cornered. A less known behavior is 'playing dead,' where a rabbit may roll onto its back and remain very still to confuse a predator or as a last-ditch effort to escape.

Rabbit communication involves a myriad of signals. Ear position can indicate mood and intent - forward for interest, laid back for relaxation or fear, and to the sides for confusion or submission. Body posture, too, conveys a lot, whether it's a content rabbit loafing comfortably or a tense rabbit crouched low, ready to bolt. Vocalizations are less common but include soft purring during contentment, growling or thumping when threatened, and a high-pitched scream when in severe distress or pain.

Understanding rabbit social structure requires recognizing the importance of companionship for these social creatures. Rabbits thrive in the company of their own kind. When kept as pets, it's often recommended to keep at least a pair, ensuring they are properly bonded to prevent territorial disputes.

However, introducing rabbits must be done carefully, following a slow 'bonding' process to prevent aggression. The hierarchy within a bonded group or pair is usually evident, with the dominant rabbit marking its territory more frequently and receiving more grooming from its partner(s).

Rabbits' complex social behavior and structure underline their intelligence, adaptability, and rich emotional life. Whether in their intricate wild societies or our living rooms, understanding and respecting these behaviors can greatly enhance our interactions with these endearing animals, providing them with a life that caters to their instinctual needs.

Chapter 3: Rabbit Habitats: Understanding, Building, and DIY Guides

Rabbits, being small mammals, have unique needs when it comes to their habitats. Both wild and domesticated rabbits are designed to live in varied environments and can be found in woods, grasslands, meadows, wetlands, and even deserts. They often make their homes in burrows, complex networks of tunnels and chambers underground, providing them shelter from predators and harsh weather conditions.

In contrast, domesticated rabbits' habitats are shaped by human care. Their needs must be addressed through the creation of a safe, healthy, and engaging living space. This includes considering their physical, mental, and social needs.

Designing a Rabbit Habitat

1. **Size**: The rabbit habitat should be spacious, allowing enough room for movement and exercise. For two rabbits, the Rabbit Welfare Association and Fund (RWAF) suggests a minimum hutch size of 6ft x 2ft x 2ft (1.83m x 0.61m x 0.61m) with an additional run area of 8ft x 4ft x 2ft (2.44m x 1.22m x 0.61m). Remember, this is a minimum; the more space, the better.
2. **Flooring**: Rabbits' paws are not adapted to wire floors, which can cause sore hocks. Choose a solid floor lined with straw, hay, or other comfortable bedding.
3. **Enrichment**: Rabbits need mental stimulation. Their habitat should contain toys, digging boxes, hiding places, and chewable items to support their natural behaviors.
4. **Safety**: The habitat should be secure from potential predators and far from harmful substances or electrical wires that rabbits might chew.

DIY Rabbit Habitat

Building your rabbit habitat can be a rewarding project. The key is to ensure it's safe, comfortable, and stimulating for your rabbits.

Materials

1. Untreated wood for the frame (2x4s, plywood for the floor and roof).
2. Wire mesh for the walls (small gauge, to prevent rabbits from escaping and predators from entering).
3. Hinges and locks for the doors.
4. Waterproof, non-toxic paint for the exterior.
5. Straw or hay for bedding.
6. Rabbit-safe toys for enrichment.

Procedure

1. **Frame Construction**: Build a rectangle using 2x4s, with dimensions 6ft x 2ft for the base. Repeat for the top frame. Connect the top and bottom with four 2ft long 2x4s at the corners, creating a box shape.
2. **Floor & Roof**: Attach a solid plywood floor to the base of the frame. Similarly, secure a plywood sheet on top as a roof.
3. **Walls**: Install the wire mesh on the sides, ensuring there are no sharp edges that could harm your rabbits.
4. **Door**: In one of the walls, create a door by cutting out a section of the wire mesh. Use 2x4s to make the door frame, and attach the mesh to the frame. Install hinges and a lock.
5. **Painting**: Paint the exterior of the frame with a waterproof, non-toxic paint to protect against the elements.
6. **Interior**: Add straw or hay for bedding on the floor. Place rabbit-safe toys, a water bottle, and a food dish inside.
7. **Run Area**: Repeat the process with larger dimensions (8ft x 4ft) for the run area, ensuring it is connected to the hutch for easy access. The run area can be fully meshed (top, sides, and

bottom) for additional security.

Building a rabbit habitat can be a fun and rewarding project. Remember to place the hutch in a weather-protected area and clean it regularly to ensure your rabbits have a safe, comfortable home. The design can be modified according to your rabbits' needs, the space available, and your creativity. Ensuring your rabbits' habitat is built to cater to their natural behaviors and needs is a vital step in providing a happy and healthy life for your pet rabbits.

Resources to Guide You

Here are some valuable resources, both websites and books, to help you learn more about creating an ideal rabbit habitat and caring for your pet rabbits. Please note that the availability of these resources may change over time, so it's always a good idea to use a search engine to find the most recent and relevant resources.

Websites

1. The Rabbit House: https://www.therabbithouse.com/
2. Rabbit Welfare Association and Fund (RWAF): https://rabbitwelfare.co.uk/
3. House Rabbit Society: https://www.rabbit.org/
4. My House Rabbit: https://www.myhouserabbit.com/
5. The Spruce Pets: https://www.thesprucepets.com/rabbits-4162062
6. Pets on Mom: https://www.pets.mom.com/
7. Binky Bunny: https://www.binkybunny.com/
8. Rabbit Care Tips: https://www.rabbitcaretips.com/
9. Rabbit Pros: https://www.rabbitpros.com/
10. RSPCA Rabbit Care Advice: https://www.rspca.org.uk/adviceandwelfare/pets/rabbits

Books

1. "Rabbit Housing: Planning, Building, and Equipping Facilities for Humanely Raising Healthy Rabbits" by Bob Bennett
2. "The Rabbit-Raising Problem Solver: Your Questions Answered about Housing, Feeding, Behavior, Health Care, Breeding, and Kindling" by Karen Patry
3. "Storey's Guide to Raising Rabbits, 5th Edition" by Bob Bennett
4. "Complete Rabbit Care" by Amy Sedaris and Mary E. Cotter
5. "House Rabbit Handbook: How to Live with an Urban Rabbit" by Marinell Harriman
6. "Rabbitlopaedia: A Complete Guide to Rabbit Care" by Meg Brown and Virginia Richardson
7. "The Bunny Lover's Complete Guide To House Rabbits" by The Bunny Guy
8. "Rabbits For Dummies" by Connie Isbell and Audrey Pavia

These resources should provide you with a comprehensive knowledge base for understanding, caring for, and building the ideal habitat for your pet rabbits. Always remember to refer to multiple sources to cross-verify information and ensure you're providing the best possible care for your rabbits.

Chapter 4: Preparing Your Home for Rabbits and Educating Your Family

Bringing a rabbit home is an exciting experience. But to ensure it's a smooth transition for both you and your new pet, it's essential to prepare your home, educate your family, and take steps to keep other pets away from the new rabbits. Here's a step-by-step guide on how to do this.

Preparing Your Home

1. **Rabbit-Proofing**: Rabbits love to chew. It's crucial to protect your rabbit from hazards and protect your belongings. Ensure wires, cords, and potentially toxic plants are out of reach. Cover baseboards and furniture legs if necessary.

2. **Secure Outdoor Spaces**: If your rabbits will spend time outdoors, secure the area to prevent escape. Ensure there are no holes or gaps in fences or gates. Remove any harmful plants or substances.

3. **Create a Safe Space**: Setup the rabbit's cage or hutch in a quiet, safe area with a consistent temperature. Avoid placing it near heating or cooling vents.

4. **Provide Necessities**: The rabbit's living area should have water, food dishes, a litter box, and toys.

Educating Your Family

1. **Responsibilities**: Explain to your family that owning a rabbit is a long-term commitment. Discuss who will be responsible for feeding, grooming, cleaning the cage, and providing exercise and playtime.

2. **Handling**: Teach your family how to properly handle rabbits. They should be picked up with one hand supporting the bottom and one hand on their chest. It's important to remember that rabbits can be easily frightened or injured, so

handle with care.

3. **Behavior**: Explain that rabbits have unique behaviors. They may not like to be held, can be active at dawn and dusk, and they need quiet time.

4. **Signs of Illness**: Teach your family the signs of a sick rabbit, like changes in eating, litter habits, or behavior, so they can alert you if something seems off.

Keeping Animals Away

1. **Separation**: If you have other pets, keep them separated from the rabbit until they can be slowly and carefully introduced. Supervise all interactions.

2. **Training**: Train dogs and cats to respect the rabbit's space. Reward calm behavior and correct overly-excited or aggressive behavior.

3. **Protection**: Never leave the rabbit unsupervised with other pets or allow them to play together until you're sure they're comfortable with each other.

4. **Outdoor Safety**: If your rabbit is outside, ensure they're protected from potential predators like birds, cats, or dogs.

Preparing your home, educating your family, and ensuring the safety of your rabbits around other pets are critical steps in welcoming rabbits to your home. Remember, each rabbit has its unique personality, so be patient and flexible as they settle in and become a beloved part of your family.

Chapter 5: Common Rabbit Breeds and Their Characteristics

Rabbits come in a wide array of breeds, each with its unique characteristics, traits, and needs. Let's explore some of the most common rabbit breeds and what sets them apart.

1. **New Zealand Rabbits**: One of the larger breeds, New Zealand rabbits often weigh 9-12 lbs when fully grown. Known for their gentle and friendly nature, they make great pets. Their coat comes in white, black, red, or broken (a mix of white and another color), and they have upright ears and a round body.

2. **Netherland Dwarf Rabbits**: Known for their compact size (1.1-2.5 lbs) and baby-like features, which they retain into adulthood. Netherland Dwarfs are generally active and energetic. They have a broad range of coat colors and patterns, a compact body, short legs, and a small, round head with large, full eyes.

3. **Lop Rabbits (Holland and French Lops)**: Known for their distinctive droopy ears. Holland Lops are smaller (2-4 lbs), with a dense coat in various colors and patterns. French Lops are considerably larger (10-15 lbs), but share a similar range of coat colors. Both breeds are generally friendly and laid-back.

4. **Rex Rabbits**: Noted for their plush, velvety fur and gentle dispositions. They are medium-sized (7.5-10.5 lbs), with a wide range of colors and patterns. Rex Rabbits are known for their upright ears, broad heads, and deep chests. Their whiskers are curly due to the same gene that gives them their plush coat.

5. **Angora Rabbits (English, French, Satin, and Giant)**: Famed for their long, soft wool, Angoras are high-maintenance but rewarding pets. English Angoras (5-7 lbs) are smaller and have wool on their ears and faces. French Angoras (7.5-10.5 lbs) have shorter fur on their faces and ears. Satin Angoras (6.5-9.5

lbs) have a unique sheen to their wool, and Giant Angoras can reach up to 9 lbs or more with ample wool. Regular grooming is crucial for these breeds to prevent matting.

6. **Lionhead Rabbits**: A small breed (2.5-3.75 lbs) with a distinctive 'mane' of fur around their head, resembling a lion's mane. Lionheads are generally friendly and enjoy social interaction. Their coat can come in various colors and patterns, and despite their fluffy appearance, they require less grooming than the Angora breeds.

7. **Flemish Giant Rabbits**: As the name suggests, these are one of the largest breeds of domestic rabbits, weighing up to 20 lbs or more. They have a semi-arch body shape, long ears, and come in a variety of solid colors. Despite their imposing size, Flemish Giants are usually calm and gentle.

Each breed of rabbit has its unique traits and needs, from the petite Netherland Dwarfs to the enormous Flemish Giants. Understanding these characteristics can help prospective rabbit owners choose a breed that best fits their lifestyle, ensuring a harmonious companionship that respects the rabbit's instincts and traits.

1. New Zealand Rabbits: As one of the larger breeds, New Zealand rabbits require spacious accommodations to maintain their health and happiness. They are often loved for their calm, amiable demeanor, which, coupled with their size, makes them great for families. Despite their friendly nature, they are energetic and require regular exercise. Grooming needs are relatively minimal due to their short-haired coats.

2. Netherland Dwarf Rabbits: Although small and cute, these bunnies can have big personalities! They are known to be a bit more skittish and energetic than some larger breeds, so a calm, patient approach to handling is important. Given their active nature, they need plenty of mental and physical stimulation despite their small size. Their coats are short and require basic grooming.

3. Lop Rabbits: Lop rabbits, both Holland and French, are characterized by their signature droopy ears, contributing to their appeal. Holland Lops, with their compact size and amicable nature, are a popular choice for families. French Lops, much larger, often behave more like a friendly, relaxed dog than a rabbit! They require ample space to roam and lounge. The ears of both breeds need regular checks for any signs of infection or parasites, and grooming needs are generally moderate.

4. Rex Rabbits: Their soft, plush fur makes them particularly pet-able. Despite the velvety coat, Rex rabbits are surprisingly low-maintenance in terms of grooming. They are intelligent and inquisitive creatures, needing ample enrichment and room to explore. Being gentle and friendly, they often do well in calm households where their sociable nature can be nurtured.

5. Angora Rabbits: These breeds are a significant commitment due to the care their woolly coats require. Daily grooming is essential to prevent matting and hairballs (trichobezoars). Despite the grooming needs, Angoras are cherished for their gentle demeanor and, of course, the luxurious wool they produce. English Angoras require the most grooming due to wool on their faces and ears, while French Angoras' faces are wool-free, reducing grooming time.

6. Lionhead Rabbits: This breed's distinctive mane adds a whimsical touch to their appearance. Lionheads are generally friendly and enjoy social interaction, but they can have a sassy side, too. Despite the mane, they don't require as much grooming as the Angora breeds but will benefit from regular brushing, especially during their molt.

7. Flemish Giant Rabbits: Truly the "gentle giants" of the rabbit world, these rabbits are admired for their calm and tolerant nature. They require considerable space due to their size, both in terms of housing and exercise areas. They have a healthy appetite and will need a good supply of hay and vegetables. Grooming needs are minimal with their short, thick fur.

In summary, each rabbit breed presents its unique set of characteristics and care requirements. Prospective rabbit owners should consider these factors, including size, temperament, activity level, and grooming needs when selecting a breed. Ultimately, providing a loving, respectful, and enriching environment tailored to their breed-specific needs will ensure a healthy, harmonious life for these charming creatures.

Chapter 6: Rabbit Life Cycle: From Birth to Adult

The life cycle of a rabbit is a fascinating journey, encompassing stages from birth to adulthood, each with unique characteristics and needs.

Birth to Two Weeks (Neonatal Period): Newborn rabbits, called kits, are altricial, meaning they are born hairless, blind, and deaf. The mother, or doe, usually gives birth in a fur-lined nest for warmth and protection. In this phase, kits feed exclusively on the doe's milk, a highly nutritious substance that allows them to double their birth weight within a week.

Two to Three Weeks (Eyes and Ears Open): At about ten days, the kits' eyes and ears open, and they begin to explore their surroundings cautiously. They start to sample solid food, such as hay and pellets, but still depend heavily on their mother's milk.

Three to Eight Weeks (Weaning Period): During this stage, kits gradually transition to solid food. Weaning is usually complete by six to eight weeks, after which they are independent of the doe's milk. Their growth is rapid during this phase, and they become increasingly active and inquisitive.

Eight Weeks to Seven Months (Juvenile Period): Known as the 'teenage' phase in rabbits, juveniles are independent but not yet sexually mature. They are very active and inquisitive, requiring plenty of exercise and stimulation. Their diet should be rich in high-quality hay to support healthy growth and development.

Seven Months Onwards (Adulthood): Rabbits reach sexual maturity at around four to seven months, depending on the breed, with smaller breeds maturing earlier than larger ones. At this stage, if not already done, rabbits should be neutered or spayed to prevent unwanted litters and mitigate certain health and behavioral issues. Adult rabbits require a balanced diet, including unlimited hay, a small number of pellets, and fresh vegetables.

Senescence (Old Age): Rabbits enter their 'golden years' at around five to six years old, although it can vary depending on breed and individual health. Senior rabbits may be less active and require special care, including more frequent health checks and potentially a modified diet. With good care, rabbits can live up to 10-12 years, and even longer in some cases.

The rabbit life cycle, from helpless neonate to curious juvenile and calm adult, showcases the remarkable transformation these creatures undergo in their lifetime. Understanding these stages and their associated needs is crucial for providing appropriate care and fostering a deep, respectful bond with these endearing creatures.

Chapter 6 Continued: Rabbit Life Cycle: From Birth to Adult - In-depth Examination

Birth to Two Weeks (Neonatal Period): When born, kits are only about the size of a matchbox, completely dependent on their mother for survival. They nurse once or twice daily, usually at night. The doe's milk, rich in fat and protein, facilitates their rapid growth. The nest needs to be kept warm and secure as the newborns are unable to regulate their body temperature effectively.

Two to Three Weeks (Eyes and Ears Open): A critical phase in a kit's life, their world begins to open up. They'll start to venture out of the nest and explore their environment, albeit clumsily. Even though they begin to nibble on hay and pellets, their digestive system is still developing, making the mother's milk essential. This period also marks the beginning of social behaviors and interaction with their siblings.

Three to Eight Weeks (Weaning Period): Kits become increasingly active and social. They'll begin to eat more solid foods and gradually wean off their mother's milk. As their diet changes, their gut microbiota adapts to break down plant material, a complex process crucial for their survival as herbivores. During this period, it's essential to provide a variety of good-quality hay to stimulate gut health and tooth wear.

Eight Weeks to Seven Months (Juvenile Period): Juvenile rabbits are bundles of energy and curiosity. They are in a stage of rapid growth and need plenty of nutrition to support their development. A diet rich in fiber from hay is crucial, along with access to fresh water and a small amount of pellets. Juveniles are very playful and require mental stimulation through toys and playtime. They should also have access to a safe space for exercise to develop strong bones and muscles.

Seven Months Onwards (Adulthood): Adult rabbits are less hyperactive but remain playful and curious. Their diet should be well-balanced, consisting mostly of hay, supplemented with fresh vegetables, herbs, and a controlled portion of pellets. Regular health check-ups become essential at this stage, including dental checks as rabbits are prone to dental issues. Adult rabbits also require regular exercise for muscular and cardiovascular health.

Senescence (Old Age): Like humans, rabbits in their golden years may face health issues, including arthritis, dental disease, kidney problems, and decreased mobility. Regular veterinary check-ups become even more critical during this stage. Some senior rabbits may require a diet adjustment, often needing softer foods if they have dental issues. They might also need extra help with grooming, especially if arthritis impairs their mobility.

Understanding the life cycle of rabbits allows us to meet their specific needs at each stage of their life. By providing appropriate care, nutrition, and environmental enrichment that cater to their growth and development, we can ensure that our rabbit companions lead a full, enriched, and healthy life.

Chapter 7: Adopting vs Buying: The Pros and Cons

Adopting or buying a rabbit is a significant decision, and both options come with their own sets of advantages and drawbacks. Here, we'll delve into the pros and cons of both to help you make an informed choice.

Adopting a Rabbit

Pros:

1. **Saving a Life**: Many rabbits end up in shelters due to various reasons. By adopting, you give a second chance to a rabbit in need.
2. **Age and Health Information**: Shelters often provide information about a rabbit's age and health status, which can be beneficial when planning care and lifestyle adjustments.
3. **Behavioral Assessment**: Shelters usually assess a rabbit's behavior, helping potential adopters understand if the rabbit would be a good fit for their household.
4. **Cost-Effective**: Adoption fees are usually less than buying from a breeder and often include costs for initial medical care like spaying/neutering, vaccinations, and health checks.

Cons:

1. **Limited Choice**: You may not have a wide variety to choose from in terms of breeds, ages, or sizes.
2. **Potential Health or Behavioral Issues**: Some rabbits in shelters might have been surrendered due to health or behavioral problems, which may require extra care and patience.

Buying a Rabbit

Pros:

1. **Wide Choice**: When buying from a breeder, you have a broader

range of breeds, colors, and ages to choose from.

2. **Pedigree Information**: If you're buying a purebred rabbit, breeders often provide pedigree information, which can be important for show rabbits or breeding programs.

Cons:

1. **Cost**: Buying a rabbit, particularly a purebred from a reputable breeder, can be expensive. Additionally, the cost of initial medical care such as spaying/neutering and vaccinations will likely be your responsibility.
2. **Supporting Inadequate Breeders**: Purchasing from pet stores or irresponsible breeders can inadvertently support poor breeding practices or the overpopulation of rabbits.
3. **Lack of Behavior Evaluation**: Breeders may not provide a comprehensive behavior assessment of the rabbit, which can be challenging for first-time owners.

Ultimately, the decision to adopt or buy a rabbit should be based on careful consideration of your lifestyle, financial capabilities, the amount of time and effort you can commit, and the kind of companion you're looking for. Regardless of the route you choose, remember that owning a rabbit is a long-term commitment that should not be taken lightly.

Chapter 8: Choosing the Right Rabbit: Factors to Consider

Choosing the right rabbit is a crucial step that can greatly influence your experience as a rabbit owner. Here are some critical factors you should take into account:

1. Size: Rabbits range from small breeds like the Netherland Dwarf (2-3 lbs) to large ones like the Flemish Giant (up to 20 lbs). Larger rabbits require more space, food, and potentially, veterinary care. Consider your living conditions and the space you can allocate to a rabbit before deciding on a breed.

2. Temperament: While individual personalities can vary, some breeds are known for particular traits. For example, Rex rabbits are often friendly and intelligent, while Netherland Dwarfs can be more skittish. Think about your lifestyle and the type of rabbit personality that would fit best.

3. Lifespan: Rabbits can live up to 10-12 years, with smaller breeds tending to live longer than larger ones. Owning a rabbit is a long-term commitment, and you should be prepared for the responsibilities that come with different life stages, from energetic juveniles to potentially health-stricken seniors.

4. Care Needs: Some rabbits require more maintenance than others. For example, Angora rabbits require extensive grooming due to their long hair, while Rex rabbits need less due to their short fur. Be realistic about the amount of time you can commit to care tasks.

5. Health: Purebred rabbits can be prone to certain breed-specific health issues. For example, lop-eared rabbits are more likely to suffer from ear infections. Mixed breed rabbits tend to have fewer health issues due to greater genetic diversity. Consider potential healthcare costs and the commitment involved in managing long-term health conditions.

6. Socialization: Rabbits are social animals and often do well in pairs or groups. However, bonding rabbits can be a complex process, and not all rabbits will get along. Consider whether you have the space, resources, and time for more than one rabbit.

7. Source: Consider whether you want to adopt from a shelter or buy from a reputable breeder. Shelters often have a variety of rabbits in need of homes, and adoption supports a good cause. Reputable breeders can provide pedigree rabbits and offer advice on care and handling. Avoid pet stores, which often source from rabbit mills and may not provide healthy or well-socialized animals.

Remember, owning a rabbit should be a joy, not a burden. Considering these factors and choosing the right rabbit for your situation will ensure a happy and harmonious relationship between you and your new furry friend.

Chapter 9: Rabbit Diet and Nutrition

Understanding a rabbit's diet is essential for their overall health and wellbeing. Rabbits are herbivores and have a unique digestive system that requires a specific diet to function correctly.

1. Hay: This should be the mainstay of your rabbit's diet, making up about 70% of it. Hay is rich in fiber, which is vital for maintaining a healthy gut as it encourages regular digestion and prevents gastrointestinal stasis. It also helps with dental health, as the grinding action required to chew hay helps keep a rabbit's continually growing teeth worn down. Timothy hay, orchard grass, or other grass hays are excellent choices for adults, while alfalfa, which is richer in protein and calcium, is better suited for young, growing rabbits.

2. Vegetables: Fresh veggies should make up about 15-20% of your rabbit's diet. Leafy greens like romaine lettuce, bok choy, kale, and carrot tops are excellent options. However, be cautious with vegetables high in sugar or oxalic acid, such as carrots and spinach, and feed these sparingly.

3. Pellets: High-quality pellets can supplement a rabbit's diet, providing essential nutrients like vitamins and minerals. However, they should only constitute about 5-10% of the diet and should be fed in controlled amounts as excessive intake can lead to obesity and other health issues. Choose pellets that are high in fiber and avoid those with added sugars, seeds, or dried fruits.

4. Fruits: Fruits are a sweet treat for rabbits and should be given sparingly due to their high sugar content. Apples (without seeds), bananas, strawberries, and pears are some examples. Consider fruits as treats and use them sparingly, not exceeding 1-2 tablespoons per day for a 6-pound rabbit.

5. Water: Fresh, clean water should be available to your rabbit at all times. Hydration is key to a healthy urinary system and helps keep the digestion process smooth.

6. Foods to Avoid: Some foods are dangerous for rabbits and should be avoided. These include legumes, rhubarb, iceberg lettuce, bread, pasta, chocolate, and all processed human foods. They can cause serious digestive problems and other health issues.

Monitoring your rabbit's eating habits, weight, and fecal output can provide crucial clues to their health. Any changes or concerns should be promptly addressed with a vet. It's important to remember that dietary needs can vary based on age, health status, and lifestyle, so it's recommended to consult with a vet for personalized nutrition advice.

Chapter 10: Housing and Environment for Rabbits

Creating a suitable living environment for your rabbit is critical to their health, happiness, and longevity. Here are some key factors to consider while setting up your rabbit's housing and environment:

1. Indoor vs Outdoor: Rabbits are best kept indoors where they are safe from predators, extreme weather conditions, and diseases. Indoor rabbits tend to have longer, healthier lives and form closer bonds with their human caretakers. Outdoor housing can expose rabbits to numerous risks and is generally not recommended by rabbit professionals.

2. Size of Housing: A rabbit's cage or hutch should be spacious enough for them to move freely. At a minimum, it should be four times the size of the rabbit when fully stretched out. The housing should also be tall enough for the rabbit to stand on its hind legs without its ears touching the top. Remember, this is just the minimum requirement - bigger is always better!

3. Exercise Area: Rabbits are active animals and need several hours of exercise daily. An exercise area, ideally a bunny-proofed room or a penned-off area, should be provided where your rabbit can hop, jump, and explore. The area should be safe from dangerous items like electrical cords or toxic plants.

4. Bedding: The cage or hutch should have a comfortable area for your rabbit to rest. Bedding made from paper or aspen shavings can provide a soft area for your rabbit to lay. Avoid cedar or pine shavings, as these can be harmful to rabbits.

5. Litter Box: Many rabbits can be litter trained. A litter box lined with safe, absorbent material like paper-based litter can be placed in the cage. Avoid clumping or cat litters, as these can cause digestive issues if ingested.

6. Enrichment: Rabbits need mental stimulation to prevent boredom and destructive behaviors. Provide toys, tunnels, hideouts, and chewable items for your rabbit to interact with. Regularly change or rotate these items to keep the environment interesting.

7. Temperature: Rabbits are sensitive to extreme temperatures. They are most comfortable in temperatures between 60°F and 70°F. High temperatures can lead to heatstroke, while cold temperatures can cause hypothermia.

8. Diet: Fresh water and hay should be available at all times. Food and water dishes should be sturdy, easy to clean, and difficult for your rabbit to knock over.

9. Companionship: Rabbits are social animals and often benefit from the companionship of another friendly rabbit. However, any introductions should be done carefully to ensure compatibility.

By providing an appropriate and enriched environment, you can ensure that your rabbit lives a happy, healthy, and fulfilling life. Remember, a rabbit's environment should cater to their natural behaviors and instincts, promoting mental and physical wellbeing.

Chapter 11: Handling and Socializing Rabbits

Understanding how to properly handle and socialize your rabbit is key to developing a strong and positive bond with them. Let's explore some essential aspects of this process.

Handling Rabbits

1. **Approach Carefully**: Rabbits are prey animals and can get easily startled. Approach them slowly and gently, letting them sniff your hand first. Avoid looming over them as this can be intimidating; instead, try to get down to their level.

2. **Proper Lifting Technique**: To lift your rabbit, place one hand under its chest and use the other to support its hindquarters. Lift steadily, holding the rabbit securely against your body to provide reassurance and prevent struggling which could lead to injury.

3. **Never Lift by Ears or Scruff**: Rabbits should never be lifted by their ears or scruff. This is painful and can cause serious injuries.

4. **Support Their Hind Legs**: Rabbit's spines are fragile, so always ensure you're supporting their hind legs to prevent kicks that could lead to a broken back.

5. **Lowering Down**: When putting your rabbit back on the ground, gently lower them bottom-first. Ensure they are steady before you let go, as a fall, even from a small height, can cause injury.

Socializing Rabbits

1. **Understanding Rabbit Behavior**: Rabbits communicate using a complex language of body signals. Understanding these signals can help you interpret your rabbit's feelings and respond appropriately. For instance, a rabbit thumping its hind leg usually signals fear or warning, while a rabbit flopping onto its

side often indicates relaxation and contentment.

2. **Building Trust**: Spend time with your rabbit daily to build trust. Sit on the floor and let your rabbit approach you on their own terms. You can encourage interaction by offering treats or toys, but don't force it. Let the relationship develop at your rabbit's pace.

3. **Positive Reinforcement**: Use treats and positive reinforcement to reward desired behaviors. This could help your rabbit associate your presence with positive experiences.

4. **Introducing New People**: Introduce new people slowly and one at a time to avoid overwhelming your rabbit. Ask them to approach gently, extend a hand for your rabbit to sniff, and offer a treat if your rabbit seems comfortable.

5. **Handling Other Pets**: Rabbits can sometimes live peacefully with certain other pets, such as guinea pigs or peaceful breeds of dogs and cats, under close supervision. However, remember that this greatly depends on the individual animals' temperaments and that interactions should always be monitored to ensure safety.

6. **Introducing Rabbits to Each Other**: If you're introducing a new rabbit, do so in a neutral space to prevent territorial aggression. The process may take time, and it's normal to see some chasing or mild nipping. However, separate the rabbits if fights break out and try again later, potentially seeking professional advice.

Through patient handling and consistent socialization, you can build a deep bond with your rabbit, understanding their unique personalities and ensuring their emotional well-being.

Chapter 12: Exercise and Enrichment Activities for Rabbits

Exercise and enrichment are fundamental to a rabbit's physical health and mental wellbeing. Rabbits are active and intelligent animals that require plenty of exercise and mental stimulation to lead healthy, happy lives.

Exercise for Rabbits

1. **Free Roaming Time**: Rabbits should have at least 3-4 hours of free-roam exercise time daily, ideally split into two sessions. This time allows rabbits to run, jump, and explore, which is essential for maintaining healthy weight and strong muscles.
2. **Safe Exercise Environment**: The exercise area should be safe and secure. Indoor exercise is generally safer, away from potential predators and harsh weather conditions. Ensure the area is 'bunny-proofed', with electrical wires, toxic plants, and small objects that could be swallowed, kept out of reach.
3. **Outdoor Exercise**: If your rabbit exercises outdoors, the area must be secure to prevent escape or intrusion by predators. Never leave a rabbit unattended outdoors, even in a secure area.

Enrichment Activities for Rabbits

1. **Toys**: Provide a variety of toys for your rabbit. Toys made from hay, willow, or untreated wood are great for chewing, which helps keep a rabbit's teeth in good condition. Other options include balls, bells, and tunnels. Regularly rotate toys to maintain interest.
2. **Puzzles and Interactive Toys**: Rabbits are smart animals that enjoy challenges. Puzzle toys or toys that dispense treats when manipulated can provide both mental stimulation and physical activity.

3. **Foraging Opportunities**: Mimic a rabbit's natural behavior by providing opportunities for foraging. Hide treats or favorite foods in their hay or inside a cardboard tube or paper bag to encourage them to 'hunt' for their food.

4. **Tunnels and Hideouts**: Rabbits love to burrow and hide. Provide tunnels, boxes, or even commercially available hideouts for your rabbit to explore and feel safe in.

5. **Training**: Rabbits can be trained to perform simple tricks using clicker training or other positive reinforcement techniques. This not only provides mental stimulation but also helps strengthen the bond between you and your rabbit.

6. **Socialization**: Rabbits are social animals and enjoy interaction with their human family members. Spend time each day with your rabbit, petting them, or just sitting near them while they explore. For rabbits that enjoy the company of other rabbits, consider adopting a pair or introducing a new friend, following proper introduction protocols.

Remember, exercise and enrichment should be tailored to your rabbit's individual personality and preferences. Observing your rabbit's behavior will help you understand what they enjoy most and adapt their activities accordingly. By providing appropriate exercise and enrichment, you will contribute significantly to your rabbit's overall quality of life.

Chapter 13: Common Health Issues in Rabbits and Preventative Care

Rabbits, like any other pets, can experience a variety of health issues. Recognizing these issues and understanding how to prevent them can significantly improve your rabbit's quality of life. Here are some of the most common health problems in rabbits:

1. Dental Problems: Rabbits' teeth grow continuously throughout their lives. If not worn down through regular chewing, they can overgrow, leading to pain, difficulty eating, and abscesses. Providing plenty of hay and chewable toys can help prevent dental problems.

2. Gastrointestinal Stasis: This condition occurs when a rabbit's digestive system slows down or stops completely. It can be life-threatening and requires immediate veterinary attention. Symptoms include a lack of appetite, small or absent fecal pellets, and a bloated abdomen. Regular exercise, a high-fiber diet, and access to fresh water can help prevent GI stasis.

3. Overgrown Nails: If a rabbit's nails become too long, they can cause discomfort or even become ingrown. Regular nail trims can prevent this issue.

4. Parasites: Rabbits can be infested with external parasites like fleas, mites, or ticks, and internal parasites like worms. Regular vet check-ups can detect and treat parasitic infestations early.

5. Obesity: Rabbits that eat a diet too high in calories, especially from treats and pellets, and don't get enough exercise can become obese, which can lead to a myriad of health problems, including heart disease and arthritis. Feeding a balanced diet and ensuring regular exercise can help keep your rabbit at a healthy weight.

6. Urinary Problems: Rabbits can develop urinary problems like bladder stones or urinary tract infections. Feeding a diet high in hay and fresh veggies and ensuring your rabbit has access to fresh water at all times can help prevent urinary issues.

7. Respiratory Problems: Symptoms like runny nose, sneezing, or difficulty breathing may indicate a respiratory infection, often caused by bacteria. Keeping your rabbit's environment clean, preventing drafts, and avoiding exposure to smoke or strong chemicals can help prevent respiratory issues.

Preventative Care

Rabbit owners can take several steps to prevent these common health problems:

1. **Regular Vet Visits**: Regular check-ups by a rabbit-savvy vet can detect health issues early and prevent minor problems from becoming major ones. A general recommendation is once a year for young, healthy rabbits and twice a year for seniors or rabbits with chronic conditions.
2. **Proper Diet**: Feeding your rabbit a balanced diet of hay, fresh vegetables, and limited pellets and treats can prevent many health issues.
3. **Exercise**: Regular exercise helps keep your rabbit's weight under control, supports digestive health, and provides mental stimulation.
4. **Good Hygiene**: Keeping your rabbit's living environment clean helps prevent many diseases. Regularly clean your rabbit's cage or hutch, litter box, and food and water dishes.
5. **Grooming**: Regular grooming, including brushing your rabbit's coat and trimming their nails, can prevent a host of issues, from hairballs to overgrown nails.

By recognizing common health issues and implementing a preventative care routine, you can help your rabbit lead a long, healthy life. Remember, if you notice any changes in your rabbit's behavior or physical condition, it's important to seek veterinary advice promptly.

Chapter 14: Rabbit Grooming: Fur, Ears, Nails, and Teeth

Proper grooming is crucial to maintaining your rabbit's health and well-being. Here are some key grooming aspects to consider:

Fur Care

1. **Regular Brushing**: Brush your rabbit's fur at least once a week, and more frequently during shedding seasons. Brushing prevents hairballs as rabbits can ingest their fur during grooming. Use a soft brush suitable for rabbits or small animals.
2. **Bathing**: Rabbits should not be bathed as this can be stressful for them and can potentially lead to shock or hypothermia. Spot clean dirty areas with a damp cloth if necessary.
3. **Checking for Parasites**: During grooming, check for signs of parasites such as fleas or mites. If found, consult a vet for suitable treatment.

Ear Care

1. **Regular Checks**: Check your rabbit's ears weekly for signs of infection or mites. Indications might include redness, discharge, foul odor, or your rabbit shaking their head more frequently.
2. **Cleaning**: If the ears are dirty, use a soft cloth dampened with warm water to clean the outer ear, avoiding the ear canal. Never use a Q-tip as it could damage the ear canal.

Nail Care

1. **Regular Trimming**: Rabbits' nails should be trimmed every 4-6 weeks. Use a small animal nail trimmer and be careful not to cut into the quick (the pink part of the nail), as this can cause pain and bleeding.
2. **Handling**: Ensure the rabbit is comfortable and well-supported

when you handle them for nail trims. It might be helpful to have another person hold the rabbit while you trim.

Teeth Care

1. **Regular Checks**: Regularly check your rabbit's front teeth (incisors) for signs of overgrowth or misalignment. Their top and bottom teeth should meet and wear each other down naturally.
2. **Diet**: A proper diet of hay, which requires a lot of chewing, can help keep a rabbit's teeth naturally trimmed.
3. **Veterinary Care**: If your rabbit's teeth seem overgrown or if they have difficulty eating, consult a vet immediately. The vet can file down overgrown teeth if necessary.

Grooming is a fundamental part of rabbit care and provides an excellent opportunity to bond with your pet while also checking for any potential health issues. It's important to familiarize yourself with each aspect of rabbit grooming and to be gentle and patient, as rabbits can be easily stressed. If you're unsure about any aspect of grooming, consult with your vet or a professional groomer experienced with rabbits.

Chapter 15: The Importance of Rabbit Neutering/ Spaying

Neutering (in males) or spaying (in females) rabbits, also known as desexing, is an essential aspect of responsible rabbit ownership. Here are some reasons why:

Health Benefits

1. **Reduced Risk of Diseases**: Spaying female rabbits significantly reduces the risk of uterine, ovarian, and mammary cancers, which are sadly common in unspayed rabbits. Neutering male rabbits eliminates the risk of testicular cancer.
2. **Longer Lifespan**: On average, desexed rabbits tend to live longer, healthier lives because of the reduced risk of certain diseases.

Behavioral Improvements

1. **Decreased Aggression**: Hormones can cause rabbits, particularly males, to become territorial and aggressive. Neutering can reduce these aggressive behaviors, leading to more sociable, friendly pets.
2. **Reduced Destructive Behavior**: Hormonal rabbits often display behaviors such as chewing, digging, and spraying urine. Desexing can significantly reduce these destructive behaviors.
3. **Easier Litter Training**: Desexed rabbits often find it easier to adapt to litter training, contributing to a cleaner and more hygienic environment.

Population Control

1. **Prevents Overpopulation**: Rabbits are renowned for their fast breeding capabilities. By neutering/spaying your rabbits, you can contribute to preventing the overpopulation of unwanted

rabbits and the related animal welfare issues.

When to Neuter/Spay

Rabbits can be desexed once they reach sexual maturity. For females, this is typically around 4-6 months of age, while males can usually be neutered slightly earlier, around 3-5 months. It's crucial, however, to consult with a veterinarian experienced with rabbits to determine the most appropriate timing for your specific pet.

Post-Surgery Care

Following surgery, rabbits usually recover quickly. It's important to keep them in a clean, quiet environment and monitor them for any signs of pain or discomfort. Regular post-operative vet check-ups are essential to ensure a smooth recovery.

Neutering/spaying is a relatively safe procedure with many benefits. It's important to consult with a veterinarian to discuss the procedure, its risks, and its benefits. Desexing is an investment in your rabbit's long-term health and well-being and can greatly enhance the bond between you and your pet.

Chapter 16: Aging Rabbits: Special Care and Considerations

As your rabbit ages, their needs and behaviors may change, and they may require additional care and attention. Here are some considerations for the care of aging rabbits:

1. Dietary Adjustments

As rabbits age, their digestive system can become less efficient, and they may struggle to maintain their weight. Your vet might recommend a diet with higher fiber content or additional supplements. Dental problems are common in older rabbits, so monitoring your rabbit's eating habits becomes crucial.

2. Increased Veterinary Care

Senior rabbits should have veterinary check-ups more frequently, ideally every six months. These check-ups can catch common age-related conditions early, like arthritis, dental disease, or kidney problems.

3. Changes in Activity Levels

Aging rabbits may be less active and spend more time resting. While it's normal for activity levels to decrease, sudden or drastic changes should be reported to your vet as they could indicate illness or discomfort. Despite reduced activity, ensure your rabbit still has opportunities for gentle exercise to maintain muscle tone and digestive health.

4. Monitoring Mobility

Joint problems and arthritis are common in older rabbits. Look for signs of decreased mobility, such as difficulty hopping, stiffness, or reluctance to move. If your rabbit has arthritis, they might benefit from soft bedding, a more easily accessible litter box, or ramps to help them get around. Your vet may suggest pain relief or joint supplements.

5. Grooming

Elderly rabbits might struggle with grooming, leading to a matted coat or overgrown nails. Regularly brushing your rabbit and helping them with their grooming becomes more important as they age.

6. Environmental Modifications

Adjust your rabbit's living environment as needed. They may benefit from a single-level habitat if they previously had a multi-level one, or from additional heating in colder months.

7. Mental Stimulation

Keep your rabbit mentally stimulated with toys, interaction, and gentle play. Mental enrichment helps maintain your rabbit's cognitive function and quality of life.

8. Compassionate End-of-Life Care

As your rabbit reaches the end of their life, they may require palliative care, including pain management, special feeding, and additional comfort measures. A veterinarian can guide you through this process to ensure your rabbit's final days are comfortable and dignified.

Aging is a natural process, and with a little extra care and attention, your senior rabbit can enjoy their golden years in comfort and happiness. Your rabbit has given you many years of companionship, and they deserve to be cared for lovingly in return as they age.

Chapter 17: Wild Rabbits vs Domestic Rabbits

While wild rabbits and domestic rabbits are both members of the same family (Leporidae), they have distinct differences in their behavior, lifestyle, and adaptation to human interaction. Here are some key distinctions:

Origins and Species

Domestic rabbits originate from the European rabbit species (Oryctolagus cuniculus). Over centuries, selective breeding has resulted in a wide variety of breeds, sizes, and colors.

In contrast, wild rabbits in North America, for example, often belong to different species like the Eastern cottontail (Sylvilagus floridanus). These species are different from the European rabbit and have not been subjected to the same selective breeding.

Behavior and Lifestyle

Wild rabbits are crepuscular, meaning they are most active during dawn and dusk. They live in complex burrow systems, known as warrens, and have a diet consisting of grasses, leaves, and some woody plants.

Domestic rabbits, while also primarily crepuscular, can adjust their schedules to align more closely with their human caretakers. Their diet consists of hay, vegetables, and specially formulated rabbit pellets.

Survival and Adaptation

Wild rabbits have adapted to survive in their natural habitats, avoiding predators and sourcing food. They are typically more alert, fast, and skittish than their domestic counterparts.

Domestic rabbits, on the other hand, depend on human care for survival. They're often less wary and more social towards humans but lack the necessary survival skills to thrive in the wild. It's important to note that domestic rabbits should never be released into the wild, as they are ill-equipped to survive and can disrupt local ecosystems.

Lifespan

A wild rabbit's lifespan is typically much shorter than that of a domestic rabbit, often only 1-2 years, due to factors like predation and disease. In contrast, with proper care, domestic rabbits can live 8-12 years or longer.

Interaction with Humans

Wild rabbits are not accustomed to human interaction and are likely to experience extreme stress if captured or handled by humans. Domestic rabbits, however, have been bred for centuries to live alongside humans and can make friendly, interactive pets.

In conclusion, while they may look similar at first glance, wild and domestic rabbits have substantial differences. It's crucial to respect these differences and never attempt to "domesticate" a wild rabbit or release a domestic rabbit into the wild.

Chapter 18: Rabbits in Different Cultures and History

Rabbits have been part of human history and culture for millennia, with a variety of symbolic representations across different societies.

Ancient Cultures

1. **Egyptian**: In Ancient Egypt, rabbits were linked to the concept of rebirth and resurrection, tying to their prolific breeding.
2. **Roman**: In Roman culture, rabbits symbolized love, sexuality, and fertility, often associated with Venus, the goddess of love.

Middle Ages and Early Modern Period

1. **European Folklore**: In Medieval Europe, rabbits were associated with fertility and spring renewal. The Easter Bunny tradition, a rabbit bringing Easter eggs, stems from these early pagan traditions of celebrating spring.
2. **Alchemy**: In alchemical texts, the rabbit was a symbol of hermaphroditism (union of opposites), due to a historical misconception that rabbits could reproduce asexually.

Asian Cultures

1. **Chinese**: In Chinese folklore, there is a Moon Rabbit (or Jade Rabbit) that lives on the moon, accompanying the moon goddess Chang'e and making elixirs of immortality. The image of the rabbit in the moon can also be found in Japanese and Korean folklore.
2. **Indian**: In one of the Jataka tales related to previous lives of Buddha, Buddha was a selfless rabbit who offered himself as a meal to a starving man.

Modern Representations

1. **Literature and Film**: Rabbits have been characters in many modern literary and cinematic works, representing various traits from cleverness and bravery (Peter Rabbit, Watership Down) to madness and chaos (the White Rabbit in Alice in Wonderland).
2. **North American Folklore**: The Br'er Rabbit tales from African-American folklore portray the rabbit as a trickster figure, using his wits to overcome adversaries.
3. **Mascots and Logos**: Rabbits are often used as mascots or in logos due to their positive associations with luck (e.g., the Rabbit's foot), speed, and fertility.

Throughout history, rabbits have held diverse meanings in various cultures, ranging from symbols of fertility and rebirth to representations of self-sacrifice or trickery. These versatile and enigmatic creatures continue to captivate our imagination in the present day.

Chapter 19: Record-Breaking Rabbits: Size, Lifespan, and More

Rabbits, while small and unassuming in general, have some impressive record holders that challenge our usual perceptions of these animals. Here are some notable record-breaking rabbits:

1. Size

The title of the world's largest rabbit has been held by a few remarkable rabbits, most of them belonging to the Continental Giant breed. The most famous was probably Darius, who measured a whopping 4 feet 4 inches long.

2. Lifespan

While the average lifespan of a domestic rabbit is around 8-12 years, the record for the oldest rabbit was held by a pet rabbit named Flopsy, who lived to be 18 years and 10 months old in Tasmania, Australia.

3. Litter Size

A New Zealand rabbit named Matilda holds the Guinness World Record for giving birth to the largest litter of bunnies. In 1978, she gave birth to 24 kits, although, sadly, not all survived.

4. Jumping

Rabbits can jump surprisingly high and far, and there's even a sport called rabbit show jumping or "kaninhop" that originated in Sweden. The highest rabbit jump record is 3.3 feet, and the longest jump record is nearly 10 feet, both held by a Danish rabbit named Tösen.

5. Breeds

As of the latest count, the American Rabbit Breeders Association (ARBA) recognizes 50 distinct breeds of rabbits. The British Rabbit Council (BRC) recognizes even more, over 60 breeds. This makes the rabbit one of the most varied species in terms of breed diversity.

6. Popularity as Pets

Rabbits are incredibly popular pets around the world. In the United States, they're the third most popular pet after cats and dogs. In the UK, they're the fourth most popular.

These records illustrate the diversity and remarkable capabilities of rabbits, from their size and longevity to their athletic abilities and popularity. Rabbits are full of surprises and continue to captivate us with their charm and unexpected talents.

Chapter 20: Rabbit Language and Communication: Understanding Binkies, Thumps, and More

Rabbits have a unique language of their own, expressed through a combination of sounds, body movements, and postures. Understanding these can help you better comprehend your rabbit's feelings and needs.

1. Binkies

A binky is a joyous expression where a rabbit jumps into the air and twists its head and body in opposite directions (sometimes in mid-air). It's a delightful display of happiness and contentment.

2. Thumps

Rabbits thump or stamp their hind legs on the ground when they sense danger or feel threatened. It's a way of warning others in their group. A thumping rabbit might be scared and need reassurance.

3. Ears

Rabbit ears are expressive. Upright ears indicate alertness or interest, while ears laid back against the body can show submission or fear. If one ear is forward and one is back, the rabbit is unsure about its environment.

4. Purring

Yes, rabbits purr! It's not like a cat's purr but a gentle teeth chattering or grinding when they're content, often during petting.

5. Nudging

If a rabbit nudges you with its nose, it may want your attention or affection, or it could be asking you to move out of the way.

Chapter 21: Rabbits and Other Pets: Can They Get Along?

Rabbits can sometimes live harmoniously with other pets, such as cats, dogs, and guinea pigs. However, their compatibility largely depends on the individual personalities, the type of the other pet, and the level of socialization and supervision provided. Here are some general considerations:

1. Rabbits and Dogs

Some dog breeds have a high prey drive and may not be suitable to live with rabbits. However, with proper introduction and constant supervision, dogs and rabbits can learn to get along. Dogs should be trained to understand that the rabbit is a member of the family, not a toy or prey. Always supervise their interactions and never leave them alone together.

2. Rabbits and Cats

Cats and rabbits can sometimes coexist peacefully, as both have similar sleep cycles and can have compatible personalities. However, cats also have a prey instinct, and they should always be supervised when around rabbits. Make sure that the rabbit has a safe, cat-free area to retreat to if necessary.

3. Rabbits and Birds

Birds should never be left unsupervised with rabbits, as they can peck and harm each other. Birds can cause significant injury to a rabbit's eyes or ears, and a frightened rabbit could inadvertently harm a bird.

4. Rabbits and Guinea Pigs

Although they are both small and often lumped together, rabbits and guinea pigs have different dietary needs and ways of communicating, which can lead to misunderstandings. Also, a rabbit can seriously injure a guinea pig accidentally during play. It's generally better to pair rabbits with other rabbits and guinea pigs with other guinea pigs.

5. Rabbits and Other Rabbits

Rabbits are social creatures and often enjoy the company of their own kind. However, introductions should be done slowly and in neutral territory to avoid territorial disputes. Spaying/neutering is crucial to prevent breeding and reduce aggressive behaviors.

In conclusion, while it's possible for rabbits to coexist with other pets, always prioritize the safety and well-being of all animals involved. Supervise all interactions and make sure each pet has a safe space where they can retreat to.

Chapter 22: The Myth of Rabbits as Low-Maintenance Pets

Rabbits are often perceived as low-maintenance pets, suitable for children or as an easier alternative to dogs or cats. However, this couldn't be further from the truth. Rabbits require specific care and attention to thrive, and the commitment to rabbit ownership can span a decade or more. Here are some areas where rabbits need special attention:

1. Diet

Rabbits need a balanced diet of hay, fresh vegetables, and limited pellets. They cannot vomit, so their diet is crucial in preventing gastrointestinal issues. The diet should be adjusted based on the rabbit's age, size, and health status.

2. Housing

Rabbits need space to run, jump, and play. Cages sold in pet stores are often too small. Also, wire-bottom cages can harm a rabbit's feet. Ideally, rabbits should have access to a bunny-proofed room or a large pen.

3. Exercise and Enrichment

Rabbits are intelligent and active animals that require daily exercise and mental stimulation. Without appropriate outlets for their energy and curiosity, rabbits can become bored and depressed.

4. Veterinary Care

Rabbits need regular vet check-ups from a rabbit-savvy vet, which can be more challenging to find than a cat or dog vet. They should also be spayed/neutered to prevent health and behavioral issues.

5. Social Needs

Rabbits are social animals and need interaction with their human caretakers and ideally, other rabbits. Loneliness can lead to depression and poor health.

6. Lifespan

Rabbits can live to be 8-12 years old, similar to many dogs and cats. Prospective owners must be prepared for a long-term commitment.

7. Handling

Unlike dogs and cats, most rabbits do not appreciate being picked up and carried as it simulates being caught by a predator. Interaction with a rabbit usually involves being on their level on the floor.

The myth of rabbits being low-maintenance pets is a harmful misconception that leads to many rabbits being neglected or abandoned. Rabbits are a significant commitment and should only be taken on by those prepared to meet their specific needs and invest time and resources into their care.

Chapter 23: Debunking the Carrot-Only Diet for Rabbits

Thanks to popular culture, notably the cartoon character Bugs Bunny, many people believe that rabbits primarily eat carrots. However, this is a widespread misconception, and a carrot-only diet can be harmful to rabbits.

1. Dietary Needs of Rabbits

A balanced rabbit diet consists primarily of hay, which should make up 70-80% of their diet. Hay is vital for their dental and digestive health. They also need a variety of leafy greens (about a packed cup per 2 pounds of body weight) and a small amount of high-fiber pellets.

2. Carrots in a Rabbit's Diet

Carrots are high in sugars and should only be given as a treat in small amounts, not as a staple of their diet. Feeding too many carrots can lead to obesity, digestive problems, and other health issues like dental disease.

3. Risks of a Carrot-Only Diet

A carrot-only diet is deficient in several critical nutrients, including the fiber that rabbits need for proper digestive functioning. It can also lead to dangerous weight gain and other health problems due to the high sugar content in carrots.

4. Ideal Treats for Rabbits

While carrots can be a small part of a rabbit's diet, other healthier treat options include small quantities of fruits like apples, bananas, and strawberries. Remember, these should be given sparingly due to their high sugar content.

In conclusion, carrots should not be the main food source for rabbits. Instead, a balanced diet of hay, vegetables, and limited pellets will keep your rabbit healthy and happy. As with any pet, before making any significant changes to your rabbit's diet, it's best to consult with a veterinarian.

Chapter 24: Misconceptions About Rabbits and Bathing

A common misconception about rabbit care is the necessity of bathing. Contrary to this belief, rabbits are meticulously clean animals that self-groom and usually do not require traditional baths. Here's why:

1. Stress and Fear

Water baths can be incredibly stressful and scary for rabbits. They're not natural swimmers and can panic when immersed in water. This stress can potentially lead to injury or shock, which can be fatal in extreme cases.

2. Risks of Hypothermia

Rabbits have a dense fur coat that takes a long time to dry. If a rabbit's fur stays damp, it can lead to hypothermia. Rabbits are very susceptible to temperature changes and do not cope well with being cold.

3. Skin Problems

Wetting a rabbit's fur can strip essential oils from their skin, leading to dryness and irritation. It can also create a damp environment where fungus or bacteria can flourish, leading to skin infections.

So, how can you keep your rabbit clean?

1. Spot Cleaning

If your rabbit gets into something messy, use a damp cloth to clean the soiled area. Make sure to dry them thoroughly.

2. Brushing

Regular brushing keeps your rabbit's fur clean, prevents matting, and reduces the risk of hairballs. It can also be a bonding experience for you and your bunny.

3. Healthy Diet

A good diet promotes a healthy coat and skin, reducing the chances of your rabbit getting dirty.

4. Litter Training

Rabbits can be trained to use a litter box, which can keep them cleaner.

In conclusion, bathing a rabbit in the traditional sense is unnecessary and potentially harmful. Always consult with a vet or rabbit expert if you're unsure about how to keep your rabbit clean and healthy.

Chapter 25: Myths About Rabbits Living Alone

Rabbits are often thought of as solitary creatures, perhaps due to their quiet nature and how they're often kept in separate cages in pet stores. However, this is far from the truth. Here's what you need to know about the social nature of rabbits:

1. Social Animals

Rabbits are highly social animals in the wild, living in groups known as warrens. They engage in social activities such as grooming each other, eating together, and participating in mutual defense.

2. Companionship Needs

In captivity, rabbits continue to have strong social needs. They can form deep bonds with their owners, but human interaction often does not fully substitute the companionship of another rabbit. Rabbits can become lonely and depressed without the company of their own kind.

3. Bonding Rabbits

Introducing a new rabbit should be done carefully, ideally in a neutral territory to avoid territorial disputes. Neutering/spaying is crucial to prevent breeding and reduce aggressive behaviors. Once bonded, rabbits can provide each other with companionship, grooming, and warmth.

4. Individual Cases

While most rabbits benefit from the companionship of their own species, individual cases may vary. Some rabbits might prefer human company or may not get along well with other rabbits due to past experiences or personality differences. Always pay attention to your rabbit's behavior to understand their needs better.

In conclusion, it's a myth that rabbits prefer to live alone. With the right introduction and care, having more than one rabbit can contribute to their happiness and overall well-being. Always consult with a rabbit-savvy vet or expert for advice tailored to your specific circumstances.

Chapter 26: Misconceptions About Rabbit Lifespan and Breeding

There are many misconceptions about the lifespan and breeding habits of rabbits, which can lead to misguided care or irresponsible pet ownership. Here are a few important clarifications:

1. Rabbit Lifespan

Many people believe rabbits have short lifespans, similar to smaller rodents like hamsters or mice. In fact, rabbits live much longer, with an average lifespan of 8-12 years for many breeds, and some can live even longer with proper care. This is a significant commitment, similar to adopting a cat or a dog.

2. Rabbit Breeding

The phrase "breed like rabbits" isn't entirely off-base—rabbits are prolific breeders. Female rabbits, called does, can have multiple litters per year, each consisting of 1-14 babies (kits). However, the rapid reproduction of rabbits should not be taken lightly.

Pet overpopulation is a serious issue, and thousands of rabbits end up in shelters each year. Moreover, uncontrolled breeding can lead to health issues for the doe, such as uterine cancer, and make it difficult for pet owners to provide proper care for all their animals.

3. Importance of Spaying and Neutering

For these reasons, it's crucial to spay or neuter pet rabbits. This not only prevents unwanted litters but can also eliminate many health risks and improve behaviors related to hormones, such as aggression or territorial marking.

4. Age at First Breeding

Another misconception is that rabbits can breed at a very young age. While rabbits reach sexual maturity relatively quickly (4-6 months for many breeds), it's not healthy or ethical to allow a rabbit to breed at this age. They are still growing themselves and are not ready for the physical toll of pregnancy.

Understanding the truth behind these common misconceptions can help rabbit owners provide the best care for their pets and contribute to responsible pet ownership. Rabbits are a long-term commitment and need careful population control to ensure each animal receives the love and care it deserves.

Chapter 27: Famous Fictional Rabbits and Their Origins

Rabbits have been a popular choice for fictional characters in literature, film, and cartoons. These characters often personify traits typically associated with rabbits, like timidity, trickiness, or speed. Here are some of the most famous fictional rabbits and their origins:

1. Bugs Bunny

Bugs Bunny, the wise-cracking rabbit from the Looney Tunes and Merrie Melodies series by Warner Bros., first appeared in 1940. With his catchphrase "Eh... What's up, doc?", Bugs is known for his cleverness and ability to outwit his adversaries.

2. Peter Rabbit

Created by Beatrix Potter, Peter Rabbit first appeared in 'The Tale of Peter Rabbit' in 1902. The mischievous rabbit, known for his adventures in Mr. McGregor's garden, is a beloved character in children's literature.

3. The White Rabbit and the March Hare (Alice in Wonderland)

These characters from Lewis Carroll's 'Alice's Adventures in Wonderland' (1865) represent the whimsical and often chaotic nature of Wonderland. The White Rabbit, perpetually late, draws Alice into Wonderland, while the March Hare hosts an ongoing tea party with the Mad Hatter.

4. Thumper (Bambi)

Thumper is the lovable rabbit from Disney's 'Bambi' (1942). He is known for his cheerful disposition and for thumping his hind foot, a typical rabbit behavior.

5. The Velveteen Rabbit

In Margery Williams' 'The Velveteen Rabbit' (1922), a stuffed rabbit yearns to become real through the love of his owner. It's a touching tale about the transformative power of love and belief.

6. Roger Rabbit

Roger Rabbit is a comedic and somewhat frantic character from the innovative live-action/animation hybrid film 'Who Framed Roger Rabbit' (1988).

7. The Rabbit of Caerbannog (Monty Python and the Holy Grail)

In the 1975 film 'Monty Python and the Holy Grail,' the Rabbit of Caerbannog is a humorously deadly creature guarding a cave. It's a play on the harmless perception of rabbits.

These famous rabbits have captivated audiences for generations, proving the enduring charm of these animals in our stories and myths.

Chapter 28: The Mystery of the Easter Bunny: Why Is It a Rabbit?

The Easter Bunny is a popular symbol of Easter, known for delivering chocolate eggs and other treats to children. However, the association of a rabbit with a Christian holiday may seem unusual. Here's how the Easter Bunny came to be:

1. Pagan Roots

The origins of the Easter Bunny have been traced back to pre-Christian fertility lore. The rabbit or hare was a symbol of abundant new life in ancient times, and springtime was considered a season of fertility, associated with new vegetation and prolific animal breeding. This symbol likely became integrated into Christian celebrations of Easter, a holiday that commemorates resurrection and new life.

2. Eostre's Hare

One theory suggests that the hare was the sacred animal of Eostre (or Ostara), the Anglo-Saxon goddess of spring and fertility. A popular story tells of Eostre transforming a bird into a hare that could still lay eggs, thus explaining the Easter Bunny's egg-delivering duties.

3. Osterhase

The specific tradition of the "Easter Hare" seems to have originated among German Lutherans. The "Osterhase" or Easter Hare, was believed to lay a nest of colored eggs for good children. German immigrants likely brought the custom to America in the 1700s.

4. Eggs and Rabbits: Symbols of New Life

Both eggs and rabbits are potent symbols of fertility and new life. Eggs have been used in fertility rites and have been viewed as symbols of rebirth for centuries, adopted by Christians as a symbol of the resurrection. The rabbit's high reproduction rate makes it a fitting symbol of spring's arrival and new life.

Thus, the Easter Bunny seems to have its roots in ancient fertility lore, adopted and adapted through the centuries, and finally commercialized into the candy-bearing hare we know today. It's an intriguing example of how symbols evolve over time and across cultures.

Chapter 29: Rabbits in Folklore and Superstition: The Rabbit's Foot and More

Rabbits have been a part of folklore and superstition across many cultures for centuries. Their habits, appearance, and unique characteristics have made them symbols of various concepts and beliefs. Here are a few examples:

1. The Rabbit's Foot

Possibly one of the most widespread superstitions involving rabbits is the rabbit's foot as a good luck charm. This belief has origins in many cultures, including Celtic and African traditions. The foot is typically carried as an amulet believed to bring good fortune.

2. The Moon Rabbit

In many East Asian cultures, the pattern of dark patches on the moon's surface is imagined as a rabbit, not a "man in the moon". This "Moon Rabbit" is often depicted as a companion to the moon goddess and is known for pounding the elixir of life in its mortar.

3. Three Hares Symbol

The three hares is a circular motif appearing in sacred sites from the Middle and Far East to the churches of Devon, England. It is thought to have a range of symbolic or mystical meanings, and has been associated with themes as diverse as the Holy Trinity and fertility.

4. Rabbit as Trickster

In some Native American tribes and African cultures, the rabbit, often an anthropomorphised hare, is a trickster figure, a clever and mischievous character in folktales.

5. Easter Bunny

As discussed in the previous chapter, the Easter Bunny is a symbol of fertility and new life that is associated with the Christian holiday of Easter.

6. Rabbits and Witches

In medieval Europe, rabbits were sometimes associated with witchcraft. It was believed that witches could transform into rabbits, enabling them to escape or carry out mischief unnoticed.

7. White Rabbits and New Months

In the UK, a common superstition involves saying "white rabbits" on the first day of a new month for good luck.

Rabbits, in their various representations, have intrigued and fascinated people, becoming embedded in our myths, stories, and superstitions. Their significance and symbolism continue to charm and captivate us, making rabbits an enduring part of human culture.

Chapter 30: The Role of Rabbits in Magic and Illusions

Rabbits have long been associated with magic and illusion. The iconic image of a magician pulling a rabbit out of a hat is deeply ingrained in our cultural consciousness. Here's how this association came about and why rabbits are often chosen for such tricks:

1. The Magic Trick's Origins

The trick of pulling a rabbit out of a hat likely originated in the 19th century. Magicians needed a trick that would surprise and delight their audiences, and the unexpected appearance of a live animal from an apparently empty hat fit the bill. The first record of such a trick is attributed to Louis Comte, a French magician, in 1814.

2. Why a Rabbit?

Rabbits are a good choice for magic tricks for a few reasons. Firstly, they're small and quiet, making them easy to hide. Secondly, they tend to freeze rather than panic when surprised, which makes them less likely to leap out unexpectedly. Finally, a rabbit's coat of fluffy fur helps to obscure the outline of its tucked-in body, enhancing the illusion that the hat is empty.

3. Symbolic Significance

Rabbits have also been chosen for their symbolic significance. In many cultures, rabbits are seen as magical and mysterious creatures, associated with transformation and trickery. This makes them a fitting choice for the art of illusion.

4. Magic and Responsibility

It's important to note that using rabbits in magic tricks carries a responsibility to ensure the animals' welfare. Stress or mistreatment can harm the rabbit, and potential magicians are encouraged to consider the rabbit's well-being first. A number of magic associations and animal welfare organizations provide guidance on this topic.

In conclusion, rabbits have played a prominent role in the field of magic and illusion. This has not only added to the enchantment of magic shows but has also contributed to the rich tapestry of symbolism and tradition surrounding these fascinating creatures.

Chapter 31: Unsolved Mysteries and Scientific Puzzles About Rabbits

Even with all the knowledge we've accumulated about rabbits, there are still areas that puzzle and intrigue scientists. Here are some of the unsolved mysteries and scientific puzzles about rabbits:

1. The Alba Rabbit

The Alba rabbit is a genetically modified "glow-in-the-dark" rabbit that was created by splicing the green fluorescent protein (GFP) of a jellyfish into the genome of an albino rabbit. While the creation of Alba raised ethical debates, it also poses scientific questions about the potential future uses and implications of such genetic modifications.

2. Mysterious Declines in Populations

In some regions, rabbit populations have seen unexplained declines. While disease, habitat loss, and predation are often the culprits, in some cases the factors contributing to these declines are not fully understood.

3. The "Rabbit Paradox"

Rabbits have been the subject of a paradox in predator-prey dynamics. Despite having many predators, rabbit populations can sometimes flourish. Understanding the factors that allow them to maintain or increase their numbers despite high predation is a complex challenge.

4. Rabbit Diseases and Resistance

Rabbits are susceptible to various diseases, such as Rabbit Hemorrhagic Disease and Myxomatosis. There is ongoing research to understand why some populations appear to develop resistance over time, and how this resistance works.

5. Jumping and Locomotion

The precise mechanics of a rabbit's jump and its unique form of locomotion, known as saltation, are still areas of active study. Understanding the full biomechanics could have implications for fields such as robotics or prosthetics.

6. Rabbit Digestion

Rabbits have a unique digestive system and engage in cecotrophy, re-ingesting special fecal pellets for nutrient absorption. While we understand the basics of this process, the full details and implications of this system are not completely understood.

These unresolved questions show that there's still much to learn about rabbits. As we continue to explore these puzzles, we'll undoubtedly gain even more respect and admiration for these fascinating creatures.

Chapter 32: Emphasizing the Joy and Responsibility of Rabbit Ownership

Rabbits make delightful companions. They are intelligent, social, and full of personality. However, it's important to understand that owning a rabbit comes with considerable responsibilities. To fully enjoy the experience and ensure the welfare of your pet, here are a few key points to consider:

1. Rabbits Have Long Lifespans

Unlike smaller rodents, rabbits have a relatively long lifespan. A well-cared-for house rabbit can live for up to 10-12 years. This means that adopting a rabbit is a long-term commitment, comparable to adopting a dog or cat.

2. Rabbits Need Space and Exercise

Rabbits need space to move and explore. They are not meant to be confined to a small cage all day. A hutch or cage should be a rabbit's safe place, not their only living space. Rabbits need daily exercise and mental stimulation.

3. Rabbits Have Specific Dietary Needs

Rabbits require a diet that is high in fiber. A proper rabbit diet consists mainly of unlimited hay, a small amount of fresh vegetables, and a limited number of pellets. Sweets, even fruits, should only be given occasionally as treats.

4. Rabbits Require Regular Veterinary Care

Rabbits need regular vet check-ups, and they should be spayed or neutered. Not all vets have experience with rabbits, so it's crucial to find a rabbit-savvy vet.

5. Rabbits Are Social Animals

Rabbits are very social and do best with a companion. A lonely rabbit can become depressed. However, introducing rabbits, especially adults, must be done carefully to ensure they get along.

6. Rabbits Aren't Always Great with Kids

Rabbits can be delicate, and improper handling can cause injury. They also can be easily frightened by loud noises. Therefore, they may not be the best pet for a young child.

7. Rabbits Can Be Trained

Rabbits are intelligent and can be trained to use a litter box and to do tricks, making them more similar to dogs and cats than people often realize.

In conclusion, rabbits can bring immense joy to their owners. However, they require time, financial resources, and a long-term commitment. Proper care and attention will ensure your rabbit leads a happy, healthy life, and in return, you'll gain a wonderful and enriching companionship.

Chapter 34: Resources for Further Information (Websites, Books, Organizations)

Rabbits are fascinating creatures, and there's always more to learn. If you're interested in diving deeper into the world of rabbits, here are some resources you might find useful:

1. Websites:

1. The Rabbit House: https://www.therabbithouse.com/
2. Rabbit Welfare Association and Fund (RWAF): https://rabbitwelfare.co.uk/
3. House Rabbit Society: https://www.rabbit.org/
4. My House Rabbit: https://www.myhouserabbit.com/
5. The Spruce Pets: https://www.thesprucepets.com/rabbits-4162062
6. Pets on Mom: https://www.pets.mom.com/
7. Binky Bunny: https://www.binkybunny.com/
8. Rabbit Care Tips: https://www.rabbitcaretips.com/
9. Rabbit Pros: https://www.rabbitpros.com/
10. RSPCA Rabbit Care Advice: https://www.rspca.org.uk/adviceandwelfare/pets/rabbits

2. Books:

- "Rabbits for Dummies" by Connie Isbell and Audrey Pavia: A practical and comprehensive guide on rabbit care.

- "The Bunny Lover's Complete Guide To House Rabbits" by The Bunny Guy: Offers in-depth information on housing, behavior, and health care for indoor rabbits.

- "Rabbit Behaviour, Health and Care" by Marit Emilie Buseth and Richard Saunders: Delivers scientific and practical information on understanding and caring for rabbits.

3. Organizations:

- House Rabbit Society: An international non-profit organization that rescues rabbits and educates the public on rabbit care and behavior.

- Rabbit Rescue Inc.: A Canadian non-profit organization dedicated to finding permanent homes for abandoned rabbits.

- American Rabbit Breeders Association (ARBA): An organization that promotes the development of the domestic rabbit and cavy industry.

Remember, learning about your pet or future pet is a continuous process. Ensuring you're knowledgeable about their needs and behavior will lead to a healthier and happier life for them, and a more enjoyable companionship for you.

First Aid For Rabbits: Basic Guidelines

Rabbits are delicate creatures, and accidents or sudden illness can occur. Having a basic understanding of first aid can help stabilize your rabbit while you seek professional veterinary care. Here are some general guidelines:

1. Rabbit First Aid Kit

Every rabbit owner should have a basic first aid kit on hand. This should include items such as gauze pads, adhesive tape, a digital thermometer, styptic powder for bleeding nails, wound disinfectant, and a basic pet-safe pain reliever as recommended by your vet.

2. Handling Injured Rabbits

Injured rabbits may be scared and more prone to struggle or bite. Gently wrap your rabbit in a towel or blanket for easier handling and to prevent further injury.

3. Checking Vital Signs

Knowing your rabbit's normal vital signs can help you recognize when something is wrong. The normal temperature for a rabbit is 101.3-104°F (38.5-40°C), and their heart rate should be between 180-250 beats per minute.

4. Bleeding

If your rabbit is bleeding, apply gentle pressure with a clean cloth or gauze to stop the blood. If the bleeding does not stop, seek immediate veterinary attention.

5. Heatstroke

Rabbits are prone to heatstroke. If your rabbit is panting, drooling, or showing signs of distress and the temperature is high, try to cool them down gradually with a damp towel and give them water. Avoid abrupt temperature changes and contact your vet immediately.

6. GI Stasis

If your rabbit has not eaten or produced feces in 12 hours, they might be suffering from gastrointestinal stasis, a potentially life-threatening condition. Offer them their favorite foods and try to get them to move around. Do not attempt to force-feed or give medications without professional advice. Consult your vet immediately.

7. Poisoning

If you suspect your rabbit has ingested something toxic, contact your vet right away. Keep the substance or a sample of the feces or vomit for testing.

8. Broken Bones

Do not attempt to set a broken bone yourself. Keep the rabbit calm and immobile and seek immediate veterinary care.

In all emergency situations, the goal of first aid is to stabilize your rabbit until you can get them to a vet. It's crucial to have a vet who is knowledgeable about rabbits, and to know their emergency contact information.

Remember, first aid is not a substitute for veterinary care. It's important to get your rabbit to a rabbit-savvy vet as soon as possible in any emergency situation.

Checklist for Rabbit Owners: Housing, Diet, Health

Becoming a rabbit owner is a big responsibility. Ensuring that your rabbit's basic needs are met can help them lead a happy, healthy life. Here's a basic checklist for you:

Housing:

- A spacious, clean cage or hutch that provides enough room for your rabbit to move and stretch freely.

- Safe bedding materials such as paper pulp or aspen shavings.

- A hidey-hole for your rabbit to retreat and feel safe.

- A litter box filled with safe, absorbent litter material.

- An environment that is kept at a safe, comfortable temperature.

- Adequate light during the day and darkness at night to mimic natural conditions.

Diet:

- Unlimited access to fresh, clean hay.
- A small portion of fresh, leafy greens and vegetables daily.
- A limited amount of high-fiber rabbit pellets.
- Fresh, clean water available at all times.
- Occasional treats, such as fruits, in moderation.

Health:

- Regular check-ups with a rabbit-savvy vet.

- An up-to-date vaccination schedule if necessary (depends on your region).

• Regular grooming sessions to check for any changes in your rabbit's skin, fur, nails, ears, teeth, and weight.

• Observing your rabbit's behavior and eating habits daily. Any changes could indicate a health issue.

• A first aid kit for emergency situations.